Scottish
Branch Lines
1955 - 65

1. At Law Junction one of the preserved Scottish locomotives No. 49 *Gordon Highlander* was in steam for a final run after six years of freedom on the main and secondary lines of the region. No. 49, preserved in Great North of Scotland livery, looked immaculate. The organiser of the tour, Roy Hamilton, is checking the timing with Grant Reid, shedmaster at Kipps, who had been looking after the locomotive.

16 October, 1965

Scottish Branch Lines 1955 - 65

by C.J. Gammell

Oxford Publishing Co.

SBN 86093 005 X

Photo reproduction by Oxford Litho Plates

Printed by Blackwell's in the City of Oxford

Photographic Acknowledgements

Acknowledgements are made, with grateful thanks, to the following for use of the photographs shown; the remainder are my own:

J. Britten: 23

L. Dench: 3, 4, 5, 7.

R. Hamilton: 12, 19, 65, 66, 71, 82, 83, 84, 85, 96, 106, 108, 110, 111, 112, 121, 123, 136, 138, 146, 153, 154.

W. S. Sellar: 2, 14, 17, 35, 36, 39, 49, 50, 63, 64, 113, 119, 120, 124, 125, 126, 129, 130, 132, 133, 134, 135, 139, 140, 141, 142, 143, 145.

W. A. C. Smith: 90, 91, 137, 163.

E. Wilmshurst: 43, 61, 74, 75, 77, 98, 148.

Published by
Oxford Publishing Co.
8, The Roundway
Headington
Oxford

Contents

The daily goods at Leslie, showing the cramped layout at this particular spot. The line closed to regular passenger traffic in 1932 and freight ceased in 1967. However, a few railtours were run in latter years.

C. H. A. Townley

Introduction

Many Scottish branch lines disappeared very rapidly during the period depicted in this book. The abolition of steam during the sixties was part of a national scheme to eliminate steam motive power from the whole of Britain. The withdrawal of steam power in Scotland was, I consider, Britain's greatest loss, for many of the minor railways of the system traversed areas of the greatest scenic grandeur. Several branch lines had always been considered vital to the livelihood of the sparsely populated areas, but with road improvements in these areas the railway was seen to be of less importance in the transport network. The Scottish Region has always been far enough away from the rest of the system to improvise some local variations of its own and it was the running of steam specials over the Region during this period that saw some of the best run steam hauled tours ever.

Each of the four preserved pre-grouping locomotives, the 'Jones Goods', *Gordon Highlander*, *Glen Douglas* and Caledonian No. 123, travelled thousands of miles in the Region during the period from 1958 to 1965. It was a sad day in 1967 when steam traction was abolished in Scotland, the quartet had travelled many miles and it was a sight not easily forgotten to see a blue, yellow, green, or dark brown engine working hard in a remote mountainous Highland area.

It has not been possible to include pictures of every station in this book but most branch lines have been included in the space available and I hope that the spirit of branch line life has been captured properly whether it be the everyday train or a rare railtour utilising ancient motive power weaving its way gingerly over weedgrown tracks.

In preparation of this book I have been greatly assisted by Bill Smith, Stuart Sellar, and the indefatigable Roy Hamilton, all of whom have been responsible at one time or another in organising many of the trains that appear in these pages.

LONDON   C. J. Gammell
September 1978

Highland

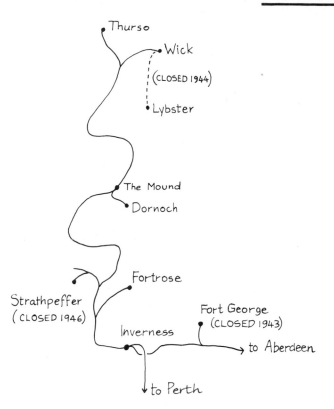

Thurso
Wick
(CLOSED 1944)
Lybster
The Mound
Dornoch
Fortrose
Strathpeffer
(CLOSED 1946)
Fort George
(CLOSED 1943)
Inverness
to Aberdeen
to Perth

The Highland main line to Britain's far north passes through magnificent scenery. The Highland Railway was not a wealthy concern but the main lines survive as they are important links with the rest of the system. Wick and Thurso, at the end of the line, are main line termini with through services to the south and cannot be considered as branch lines. The Highland Railway had a few short branch lines of which little can be seen nowadays. Over the lines in the north the famous 'Jones Goods', the first 4-6-0 engine in the country, worked special trains during the 1960s; a slow and cumbersome machine with curious gauge glasses on the boiler it would sometimes get to its destination on time, sometimes not. The resplendent yellow Highland livery of the locomotive set in the rolling mountain scenery of the Highlands was a sight to please any passer-by willing to savour the sounds of this ungainly machine plodding away over mountain passes of the former Highland main line.

3. The last Highland Railway passenger tanks in service were the tiny 0-4-4s built at the turn of the century. No. 55051 simmers at The Mound with the Dornoch branch mixed train.
27 July, 1955

◄ 2. The arrival of the daily goods at Cairntows Crossing on the St Leonards branch behind a North British 0-6-0 No. 64479.

12 August, 1961

4. The Dornoch branch was worked by trains that were 'mixed', sometimes passenger coaches and goods wagons, sometimes one passenger coach and a string of goods vehicles.

27 July, 1955

5. A passenger's eye view of The Mound from the approaching Dornoch train. The road and railway shared the causeway across to The Mound station. Traffic by road and rail was light, the gate swings over to close off road or rail depending on which system is in use!

27 July, 1955

6. Leaving Inverness the 65-year-old 'Jones Goods' sets out to explore Highland branch lines in 1962. The main line to Perth swings over to the left behind the train. In the background, behind Inverness, can be seen the snow capped mountains of the Highlands.

21 April, 1962

7. The Dornoch train pauses at Embo to pick up a few local passengers for Britain's smallest cathedral city. The station buildings at Embo are still in LMS livery in this picture. The line opened in 1902 as a light railway and closed down on 13 June, 1960. The Mound was named after Telford's embankment of 1817, constructed to take the main road and carried the railway to Dornoch from 1902 to 1960.

27 July, 1955

8. Forfar shed had an unusual resident in 1962, the last Highland Railway 4-4-0, *Ben Alder*, No. 54398. Attempts were being made to preserve this locomotive which was ideal for branch line tours. The problem was that the engine had been rebuilt with a Caledonian boiler and was not therefore the complete Drummond engine of 1898. The locomotive here photographed on 16 June, 1960, was eventually scrapped by British Railways, there being no suitable home for it.

9. The Highland Railway operated the Fort Augustus Railway but did not have any physical connection with it. This view shows the remains of Aberchalder station in 1963, the station having been converted to a private house when closed in 1933. Note the use of concrete in the engineers' work, one of the earliest examples in railway construction.

2 June, 1963

10. Avoch (pronounced 'Auch'), on the Black Isle branch with 'Caley' 0-6-0 No. 57594 on an RCTS/SLS tour in 1960. This was in fact one of the tours organised by the railway societies at the then astronomical cost of £14 for a week. This included travel over 32 closed branch lines and use of many pre-grouping types of locomotive! The Black Isle branch, opened in 1894 closed to passengers in 1951; this was the last train.

14 June, 1960

11. Highland Railway No. 103 arrives at Alves for the Burghead branch. The train ran so late that the author, waiting for the train by the side of the embankment, fell asleep on the grass and a large worm crawled into his camera! A toot from the approaching train awoke the author who quickly removed the offending worm from his camera just in time to take this picture of the train pulling in.

21 April, 1962

12. A rare event; No. 49 *Gordon Highlander* and 'Jones Goods' No. 103 swing into Craigellachie with a special in 1962. *Gordon Highlander* was a regular performer on the Speyside line before and after restoration to GNSR colours.

16 June, 1962

13. The Old Meldrum goods in the autumn of 1957 with North Eastern J72 class 0-6-0 tank on the daily goods. The branch closed to goods traffic in January 1966.

20 September, 1957

Grampian

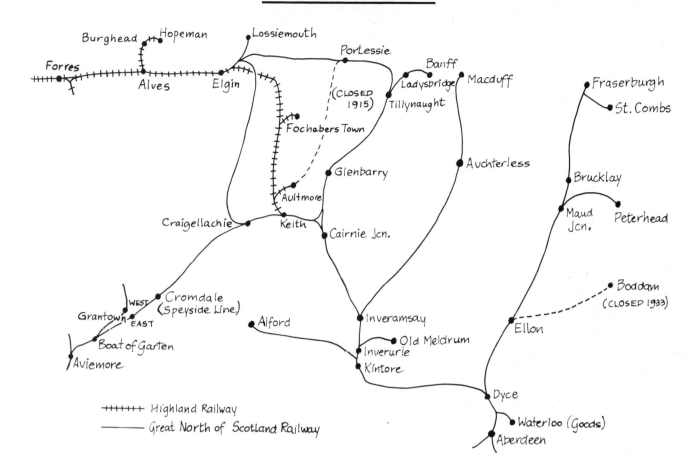

The Great North of Scotland Railway branch lines in Aberdeenshire radiated outwards from Aberdeen in a northerly direction. All passed through rural countryside with little competition from other companies except in the Keith to Elgin area of Morayshire where a curious situation existed. Here were three lines from Cairnie Junction to Elgin, two GNSR and one Highland. The Highland Railway constructed a branch line to Portessie from Keith in 1884 to rival the GNSR to the coast but the Highland line did not thrive and was lifted in 1915 from Aultmore. Although the track was removed the stations remained intact; the rails were put back after the first war by the LMS and then removed again when the line was found to be of no use. The stations still survive, a legacy from this curious rivalry between two companies.

The long branches to Macduff, Alford and Old Meldrum were still open for freight in 1960 - 1962 and saw plenty of specials; the Fraserburgh and Peterhead lines closed to passengers in 1965.

14. The Speyside line of the former Great North of Scotland Railway with a Caledonian 0-6-0 on a stopping passenger train at Cromdale. Notice the ornate spikes to the finial of the Cromdale nameboard. The Speyside line, noted for its distilleries and their branch lines worked by industrial locomotives, closed in October 1965.

15. Lossiemouth sees an ex LMS 2P 4-4-0 on the morning passenger train from Elgin. The branch closed to passengers in 1964; it handled a lot of fish traffic from the harbour.

2 May, 1958

16. Elgin (West), or the Highland side of the junction station, with No. 103, the 'Jones Goods', arriving with an Easter tour main train en route to Fochabers. The low platforms originated from the Inverness and Aberdeen Junction Railway, a constituent of the Highland Railway. Little platform stands await the detraining of the passengers, assuming that the train stops at the correct point! Stands are lettered 'Elgin (West)', 'Elgin West' or just plain 'B.R.' This was necessary to prevent the stands being taken away to the GNSR side of the station, Elgin (East) where the platforms were of normal height.

21 April, 1962

17. Grantown-on-Spey with the Speyside train again. Here bicycle traffic is being unloaded from an ex-LMS brake in early British Railways red and cream livery.

10 August, 1956

18. King Edward on the Macduff branch is in the centre of the potato growing district of Aberdeenshire. The station buildings with their ornate Victorian timberwork are ideal specimens for the modeller looking for something different. The line closed to passengers in 1951.

21 April, 1962

19. GNSR No. 49 *Gordon Highlander* on the week's tour pictured here at Alford in June 1960. An excellent example of GNSR starting signal graces the platform. Alford closed in January 1950 to passengers but was used for many years afterwards for freight.

13 June, 1960

20. Crossing the river Spey, near Orton, on the Highland
line from Elgin to Keith, the elderly 'Jones Goods' No.
103 nears the summit of the line.

21 April, 1962

21. The Old Meldrum branch is traversed by No. 49 *Gordon Highlander* during the BLS/SLS Easter tour of 1962. One of the intermediate stations, Lethenty, here pictured, shows the Great North of Scotland Railway country station with wood and brick material. An example of this type of structure can still be seen at Knockando distillery.

21 April, 1962

22. The terminus at Old Meldrum with *Gordon Highlander* right back on the buffer stops. The agricultural nature of the countryside is evident in this picture. Although closed for passenger traffic in 1931 the Old Meldrum branch did well with seed potato traffic until BR days.

21 April, 1962

23. Guard's eye view of Lethenty from the brake van of the daily goods to Old Meldrum. The red stop signal applies to road or rail depending on the position of the gates.
20 September, 1957

24. Macduff terminus sees a special train in June 1960; the line closed to passengers in 1951. On the other side of the harbour was the terminus of another branch line from Tillynaught to Banff.
13 June, 1960

25 and 26. Great North of Scotland termini shown here are Banff (above) with train shed using wooden material in the roof and Macduff (below) with stonework in roof. Both buildings have a circular smoke vent under the pediment but offer little weather protection to the travelling public as the locomotive occupies the covered area!

21 April, 1962

27. The Banff branch train with class 2 2-6-0 No. 78054 approaching Ladysbridge with well preserved wooden GNSR station buildings. The watertap on the station is a common feature on Scottish stations. The wooden station building was later used as a sports pavilion, having been moved 3 miles down the road after the branch closed in July 1964.

21 April, 1962

28. Tillynaught, the junction for the Banff branch, showing the elaborate station roofing for such a tiny junction; the locomotive is No. 78045.

25 January, 1964

29 and 30. The ex-Great North of Scotland area still had six-wheeled carriages in use in one form or another right up to 1965. In the sidings at Glenbarry on 21 April, 1962 is a six wheeler used by the Civil Engineer's department as a messing van (above). At Ballater (below) on 2 May, 1958 a GNSR six wheeler has been turned into a staff dormitory van painted in green and cream livery, complete with curtains. The GNSR never scrapped its coaches, so many of these vehicles survive on farms.

31. A view of Aboyne with the Ballater branch train, worked by a class 4MT 2-6-4T complete with snow-plough. The Deeside Railway as the Ballater branch was known was opened in sections, the part to Aboyne being built by a company known as the 'Aboyne Extension' opened in 1859. The branch was opened to Ballater in 1866; it has been said locally that the line was prevented from being extended to Braemar at the wish of Queen Victoria who disapproved of a railway in the vicinity of Balmoral Castle. The Deeside line closed in February 1966.

1 May. 1958

32. Inverbervie, the terminus of the former North British line from Montrose at Easter 1962. Now in Grampian, formerly in Kincardine, the Inverbervie or Bervie branch as it was known locally, lost its passenger services in 1951. The guard and lengthman look on apprehensively thinking that this was the last train on the branch, but there were other tours later on. Note the immaculate condition of the station building. (Bervie was renamed Inverbervie in 1926).

22 April, 1962

33. A view of the Montrose to Inverbervie branch from the leading vehicle as the class J37 0-6-0 ascends the bank to North Water Bridge Viaduct with the summer 1960 railtour from Montrose.

16 June, 1960

34. Brucklay station on the Fraserburgh branch, a small country GNSR station with stonework finish and brick outbuildings. The loop has been removed, making the nearside platform redundant. Great North of Scotland stations were stone built until the turn of the century when the standard wooden type came into use.

25 January, 1964

35. Fraserburgh, the end of the line from Dyce Junction, closed in October 1965. Here the St Combs branch train is about to leave behind a LMS class 2 2-6-0, a class of locomotive that seemed to leak steam in all directions. The fine stonework engine shed blends in well with the other prominent buildings in the town.

9 August, 1956

36. A view of St Combs, the terminus of the light railway from Fraserburgh with class 2 2-6-0 No. 46461. The line, which opened in July 1903 and closed in May 1965, had an undulating course over 1 in 50 and 1 in 60 gradients across agricultural countryside. The St Combs branch was previously worked by Great Eastern F4 class 2-4-2 tank engines.

9 August, 1956

37 and 38. A rare class of locomotive was the shortlived North British type 2, 1100 hp diesel-electric in the D6100 series, here seen at work on the Peterhead branch. The North British Locomotive Co. built steam engines for many parts of the world but when it came to diesel locomotive construction the engines were not a success. The terminus at Peterhead (above) and (below) Maud with the loco running round the short train of LMS stock are seen the year before closure, actually 'Rabbie Burns Day' 1964. The lines closed in May 1965.

25 January, 1964

Tayside

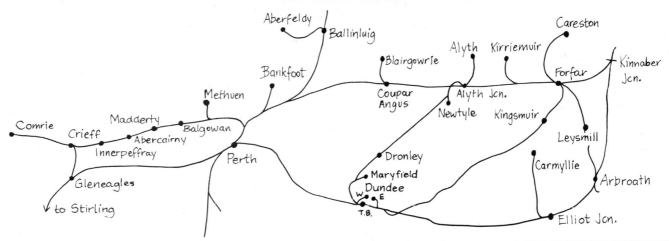

The main line from Perth to Aberdeen on which the 3 hour expresses were run with various forms of motive power, from LMS 'Black Fives' to LNER A4 class Pacifics, had many branches leaving in northerly and southerly directions. The Caledonian used to rival the North British for the Anglo-Scottish express traffic and the 'Race to the North' would start from Euston and Kings Cross respectively. Both the East Coast and West Coast lines had their own routes to Kinnaber Junction which was the vital spot in the whole race. The train that got there first won the race to Aberdeen. Today not only are the branches on the route closed but so is the main line from Perth to Kinnaber Junction.

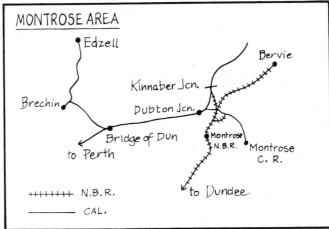

39. The daily goods from Auchterhouse to Dundee on the former Dundee and Newtyle Railway; the line closed to passengers in January 1955. The original Dundee & Newtyle Railway opened in 1831 and was the first in the north of Scotland. The line was horse worked, the gauge being 4ft 6½in, two inches narrower than the British standard.

40 and 41. The Aberfeldy branch of the former Highland Railway left the main Perth to Inverness line at Ballinluig. A Caledonian 0-4-4 tank No. 55217 is seen at Ballinluig (above) with the Inverness train arriving behind a type 2 D5300 class diesel and (below) the terminus at Aberfeldy with 'Caley' 439 class 0-4-4 tank No. 55217 of 1900. An example of this famous class of passenger tank has been preserved and can be seen at the Scottish Railway Preservation Society Headquarters at Falkirk. Aberfeldy closed to passengers on 3 May, 1965.

31 August, 1961

42 and 43. Bankfoot before and after! The 'Caley' 0-6-0T is seen (above) arriving at the terminus of the short branch from Stanley Junction near Perth on 23 April, 1962 with an SLS/BLS special. In the lower picture taken on 20 April, 1965 the remains of Bankfoot after the track had been lifted can be seen. The passenger service finished in 1931 but potato traffic lasted until 1964. The station is now a milk bar in a caravan site, the branch is built on by part of the A9 trunk road.

44. Newtyle Old, the original Dundee and Newtyle Railway terminus as viewed from the rear of a departing passenger train — a special organised by a railway society. The original station dates from 1831 and was built to accommodate trains from Dundee which had been worked by horse and cable over inclines.

23 April, 1962

45. A portrait of Alyth, the terminus of the branch from Alyth Junction on the Perth to Aberdeen main line which closed on 2 July, 1951. The cramped conditions in which passenger and goods traffic had to be dealt with is obvious. The site is now occupied by a housing estate.

23 April, 1962

46. Blairgowrie, with one of the famous Caledonian 4-4-0s No. 54465 built by Pickergill in 1916, pushing back into the platform. The station here is adorned with an overall roof of wooden construction. Blairgowrie closed to passengers in January 1955 but the station is still well preserved although the track has been lifted.
23 April, 1962

47. Caledonian 0-6-0 No. 57441 arrives at Alyth Junction before setting forth up the Alyth branch with a train which includes the two restored Caledonian coaches.
16 June, 1960

48. Caledonian 0-6-0 2F No. 57441 is seen here resting at Kirriemuir on the 1960 week's tour of Scottish branch lines organised by the RCTS and SLS. The stock behind the engine is interesting and consists of two Caledonian vehicles, one Great Eastern buffet, one BR standard and one Gresley brake. The branch closed in August 1952.

16 June, 1960

49. Brechin, with the Edzell goods paying a call with J37 class 0-6-0 No. 64587. Brechin was a terminal station for three lines, and regular passenger services finished in August 1952. The station is still very much in being.

4 March, 1961

50. The daily goods at Stracathro on the Edzell branch hauled by North British 0-6-0 No. 64587. The Edzell branch closed in April 1931 but reopened on 4th July, 1938! The line finally closed to passenger traffic on 27th September, 1938.

4 March, 1961

51. The end of the line at Careston which had an occasional freight train from Forfar. The line lost its passenger service in August 1952.

22 April, 1962

52. An unusual incident occurring on the Carmyllie branch in 1960. A LMR class 2 2-6-0 confronting a traction engine named 'Jinglin Geordie' on the Carmyllie Light railway, formerly of the Dundee and Arbroath Railway. The idea was to simulate the incident in the 'Titfield Thunderbolt' where a traction engine has a duel with the train at an ungated crossing. This crossing is unusual for a light railway in that the cattle ramps are raised and not horizontal.

16 June, 1960

53. Carmyllie station, the terminus of the light railway from Elliot Junction. Not much room for lengthy trains here! Possibly the smallest station in Scotland, with only room for a six wheeled coach, the line closed to passenger traffic in December 1929.

16 June, 1960

54. Two class 2 2-6-0s set out from Elliot Junction for Carmyllie with a five coach load, very necessary in view of the 1 in 36 gradient encountered en route. The Carmyllie branch was opened for passenger traffic in 1900, being the first railway in Scotland to be opened under the 1896 Light Railway Act.

22 April, 1962

55. Return to Elliot Junction of the special from Carmyllie, Easter 1962. The branch turnout had no platform, Elliot Junction being an island on the main line of the former Dundee and Arbroath Joint Railway (Caledonian and North British). The leading engine No. 46464, is now on Speyside for working the Strathspey Railway, Aviemore.

22 April, 1962

56. The express headcode carried by Caledonian 4-4-0 No. 54485 belies the nature of the train which is in fact an all stations local from Perth to Crieff during the SLS/RCTS week's tour of 1960. The train has stopped briefly at Innerpeffray, the last station before Crieff on the line from Perth, closed to passengers in October 1951 and completely in September 1967.

15 June, 1960

57. 'Caley' 4-4-0 No. 54485, (Pickersgill 72 class of 1920) about to move a special out of the weedgrown station at Methven in the summer of 1960. This short Caledonian branch line closed to passengers in September 1937.

15 June, 1960

58. Caledonian 4-4-0 No. 54485 en route from Perth to Crieff pauses for a few minutes at Abercairny.

15 June, 1960

59. A stranger to Caledonian branch lines was the North British 4-4-0 *Glen Douglas*, one of the four preserved engines, seen here approaching Balgowan on the Perth to Crieff line.

23 April, 1962

60. A 'Caley' 4-4-0 at Crieff on the week's railtour in June 1960. Crieff was a country junction with lines to Gleneagles (closed July 1964) and Perth.

15 June, 1960

61. The 4 wheeled railbus seen here at Comrie, was tried out on several lines in Scotland from 1958 onwards and some were used following the successful adoption of the type on the German Federal Railway. The Scottish Region used several types from British builders and even used battery railcars. Notice the wooden station nameboard.

29 July, 1960

62. Caledonian 4-2-2 No. 123 trundles over the river Tay Bridge at Perth on an evening tour of Perthshire branch lines in 1960.

16 June, 1960

63. Dundee (East), a short town branch line, the terminus of the Dundee and Arbroath Joint line. Dundee was blessed with plenty of terminals — East, West, Tay Bridge and Maryfield. Dundee (East) closed in January 1959. Here North British C16 class 4-4-2T No. 67502 prepares to shunt empty stock from this fine Victorian station, opened in December 1857.

8 October, 1958

64. The Charlestown goods worked by North British J36 class 0-6-0 No. 65253 formerly named *Joffre*. A few of the NBR 0-6-0s carried names of first world war generals, a relic from their service in France from 1914-1918. The names were gradually discontinued under BR ownership. The Charlestown goods seems to have collected only a few wagons of scrap forming an unfitted freight for Dunfermline. This line closed to passengers as early as November 1926.

11 April, 1961

65. A post grouping development of the NBR and NER 0-6-0 was the Gresley J38 class of 1926. Loco No. 65905 is seen here with an SLS/RCTS tour in 1962 at Methil East Fife. The Methil line closed to passengers in January 1955. The train has BR standard stock in maroon with the two Caledonian coaches on the rear. One Caledonian coach spent many years on the Bluebell Railway in Sussex until eventually exchanged by the Scottish Railway Preservation Society for a Bulleid all steel vehicle which had come into Scottish Region stock.

19 June, 1962

Fife

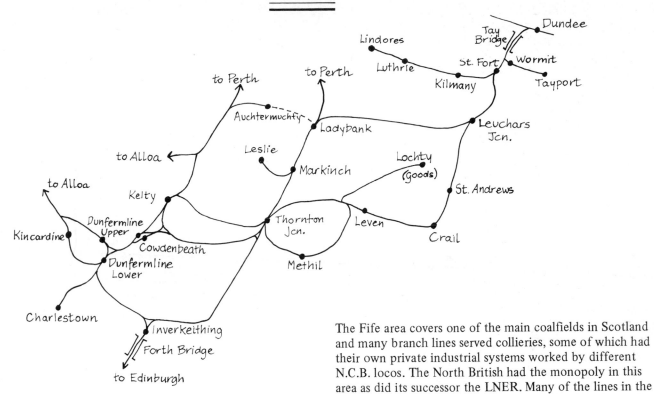

The Fife area covers one of the main coalfields in Scotland and many branch lines served collieries, some of which had their own private industrial systems worked by different N.C.B. locos. The North British had the monopoly in this area as did its successor the LNER. Many of the lines in the industrial areas still see plenty of coal traffic but the rural lines have long since closed.

66. The Lochty goods branch considered by many to be the longest goods only branch line in Scotland was operated by North British 0-6-0s with tender cabs. The picture below depicts the locomotive running round a few empty wagons. Remarkably a part of this line has been preserved as the Lochty Private Railway.

20 January, 1962

67. Tayport on 31 August, 1961. A commuter service from Dundee operated to here but with completion of the Tay Road bridge the service was withdrawn, the line closing in September 1967. Very fine lamps adorn the station and North British lower quadrant signals can be seen in use.

68. The well preserved North British 4-4-0 No. 256 *Glen Douglas* stops briefly at Crail on the week's tour in June 1960. The signalman has a little platform to stand on when collecting the token for the single line from the fireman. This line closed in September 1965.

12 June, 1960

69. The North British Railway enamel nameboard survives in this photograph of Class J39 0-6-0 No. 64786 on a special tour to this goods only branch in 1962 organised by the SLS/BLS. Lindores was the extent of the line when this photograph was taken, the line to Perth having been severed at Glenburnie Junction. The Newburgh and North Fife Railway was opened for business on 25 January, 1909 from St Fort. When British Railways announced the closure of the line in 1950, Fife County Council objected on the grounds that the line was to be operated in perpetuity by the NBR. The objection was overcome by substituting a bus service.

22 April, 1962

70. The 'Scottish Rambler' about to return from Luthrie to Perth behind Class J39 0-6-0 No 64786 of 1926. The enamel nameplates are still in position despite the fact that the line closed in 1951.

22 April, 1962

71. Charlestown again with class J38 No. 65905. All 35 engines in the class were allocated to Thornton, Dunfermline and Edinburgh St Margaret's sheds for working the coal trains.

19 June, 1962

72. North British class J37 0-6-0 No. 64618 comes to a rest at Leslie with a special. The Leslie branch closed to passengers in 1932 and freight in 1967.

3 April, 1963

Central

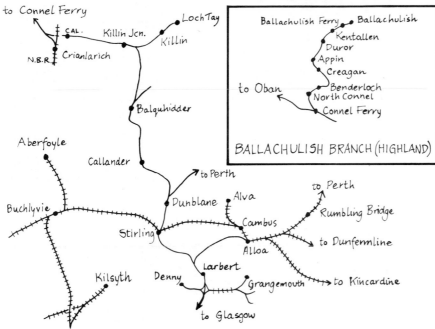

BALLACHULISH BRANCH (HIGHLAND)

The Oban line passed through some very fine mountain scenery and crossed the North British West Highland line at Crianlarich. The Caledonian Oban line had two very choice branches, one to Killin and the other to Ballachulish now both closed. The main line from Dunblane to Crianlarich has now also suffered closure as the result of a landslide in one of the glens in 1965. The North British branch to Aberfoyle was a very popular line for tourists in the summer as it went straight to the Trossachs. Alloa was a very good centre to watch steam working as apart from the many lines radiating from the town there were many colliery and trip workings from Fife.

73. Caledonian Railway No. 123 negotiates a rare piece of track at Crianlarich from the Oban line to the West Highland line in a snowstorm. The rare connection between the two lines has now become part of the main line as the Callander to Crianlarich section was closed by a landslide in September 1965.

12 April, 1963

74. The branch engine No. 55195 drops down into Killin station with a single van from the junction. The Caledonian 439 class of passenger tank introduced in 1900 were well known on Scottish branch lines of the former LMS. An example of the class, No. 419 built in 1907, is preserved in original Caledonian livery at Falkirk, headquarters of the Scottish Railway Preservation Society.

5 May, 1959

75. Killin, with 'Caley' tank No. 55195 and single coach train for the junction; the locomotive would be stabled on the branch at Loch Tay.

5 May, 1959

76. Callander, now closed, with No. 123. This venerable machine was the Caledonian Railway's Royal Train pilot engine and used to precede the main train in case there was any obstruction and to warn staff of the special to follow. This famous engine was unique, built in 1886 it was the only engine of its class and was the only 4-2-2 to run on a Scottish Railway. During the 1888 'Race to the North' No. 123 worked the expresses from Carlisle to Edinburgh in under two hours. During the 1920s No. 123 worked directors and engineers specials and in 1930 was returned to normal traffic! This was the last single wheeled engine to be used in the U.K. After withdrawal in 1935 the engine was kept safely in store until suddenly it reappeared in March 1958 on a press run from Edinburgh to Perth! From 1958 until 1965 No. 123 operated on various specials hired by clubs and even ventured as far afield as Sussex where it worked a special on the Bluebell Railway. The author had great pleasure in rostering this locomotive and crew on a special from London to Haywards Heath in 1963, diagrammed in the special traffic notice as 'Dawsholm special No. 1. The Scottish Region demanded the return of No. 123 the same night from the Southern Region just in case some ambitious roster clerk might send it off on a ballast train to Portsmouth! Alas No. 123 is once again safely secured in the Glasgow Transport Museum and on public view.

12 April, 1963

77. On arrival at Killin Junction, the crew pose momentarily before the train from Oban arrives. The branch closed on 28th September, 1965.

5 May, 1959

78. Loch Tay was the end of the line for 'Caley' 0-4-4T No. 55126. This little piece of line only had light engines on it as the passenger service was withdrawn in September 1939 when the steamer on the Loch was withdrawn. The Killin branch engine would go to Loch Tay for water in between trains.

1 June, 1957

79. Inside the engine shed at Loch Tay with CR 0-4-4T No. 55126 taking water rather laboriously through an ancient column, known to enginemen as "dropping the bag"!

1 June, 1957

80. The terminus at Ballachulish, with a 'Caley' tank nestling under the hills ready to depart for Connel Ferry. The branch was opened in August 1903 by the Caledonian Railway and finally closed in March 1966. A very fine example of Caledonian signalbox in timber with slate roof can be seen here.

1 June, 1957

81. North Connel bridge over Loch Etive as viewed from the train showing the access for both rail and road traffic. Road traffic arrived on the left, the driver paid the toll, and when the line was clear proceeded at 4 mph! When the bridge was closed the motorist had a detour of 75 miles round Loch Etive! Now that the railway has closed the bridge is free exclusively for road traffic.

1 June, 1957

82. Oban with the 4.55 pm mixed to Ballachulish about to leave with 'Caley' tank No. 55224.

8 June, 1960

83. Connel Ferry, the junction for Ballachulish, with 0-4-4 tank No. 55238 running round the 12.26 pm Ballachulish to Oban. Note the fine home signal and siding signal.

8 June, 1960

84. A Caledonian Railway 0-6-0 No. 57587 leaves Benderloch on the Ballachulish branch with a mixed freight train of stone and cement. The Ballachulish branch had a daily goods worked through from Oban.
12 May, 1962

85. A motorist's eye view of the road and rail bridge at Connel Ferry with Standard class 2 2-6-0 No. 78052 on the 10.48 am Ballachulish to Connel Ferry train. Road traffic was not permitted to cross at the same time as a train. Note the check rail for motorists to prevent them from rubbing against the chairs on the track.
12 May, 1962

86. The crew pose in front of the diesel multiple unit on the Grangemouth branch with the driver holding the single line token. The docks branch leads away to the right. This branch was closed to passengers in January 1968.

31 August, 1961

87. A Caledonian engine and train about to depart from Denny with a special for Larbert. The loco is a 'Caley' 3P Pickersgill 4-4-0 of 1916. Denny closed to regular passenger services in July 1930.

7 May, 1960

88. North British 0-6-0 No. 64569 of class J37 struggles out of Dunfermline with a coal train from one of the Fife branches in the last full year of steam working in Scotland.

28 May, 1966

89. A nice easy pace for a J38 drifting down into Alloa station with loaded coal for the Fife branches. J38s worked trips from the colliery branches to the washing plants and the line to Dunfermline was very busy with this traffic.

28 May, 1966

90. Bo'ness on the last day as No. 43141 prepares to leave with a two coach train on the 7.20 pm to Polmont. Certainly one of the quieter 'funerals', last trains were usually seen off by brass bands, provosts, and the press; Bo'ness seems to have been forgotten.

5 May, 1956

91. Aberfoyle, the Trossachs terminus with a Gresley K2 class 2-6-0 No. 61788 *Loch Rannoch* on a Glasgow University rail tour. The vehicle next to the engine is one of the LNER observation cars usually used on the West Highland line.

16 May, 1959

92. The road to the isles, a foot-plate view of the way ahead on the SLS railtour to Aberfoyle. North British class J36 0-6-0 No. 65315 is about to negotiate the weedy track near Buchlyvie.
3 May, 1958

93. Kilsyth, with a Holmes NBR 0-6-0 dating from the 1880s ready to take the train away to Aberfoyle. Regular passenger services were discontinued in August 1951.
3 May, 1958

94. Class J36 0-6-0 No. 65323 about to leave Alva with an Easter special for Fife. The passenger service was withdrawn in November 1954. This is 'Scottish Rambler No. 2' organised by SLS and BLS.

3 April, 1963

95. View from the Devon Valley train showing the elevated signalbox at Rumbling Bridge with pulleys and signal wires running across the grass. Alloa to Kinross Junction was closed in June 1964.

3 May, 1958

Strathclyde

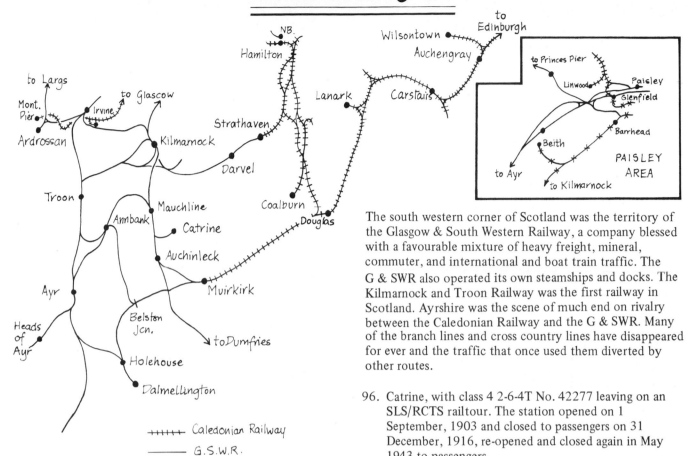

The south western corner of Scotland was the territory of the Glasgow & South Western Railway, a company blessed with a favourable mixture of heavy freight, mineral, commuter, and international and boat train traffic. The G & SWR also operated its own steamships and docks. The Kilmarnock and Troon Railway was the first railway in Scotland. Ayrshire was the scene of much end on rivalry between the Caledonian Railway and the G & SWR. Many of the branch lines and cross country lines have disappeared for ever and the traffic that once used them diverted by other routes.

96. Catrine, with class 4 2-6-4T No. 42277 leaving on an SLS/RCTS railtour. The station opened on 1 September, 1903 and closed to passengers on 31 December, 1916, re-opened and closed again in May 1943 to passengers.

20 June, 1962

97. The railbus from Lugton pauses at Beith Town; it is an A.C. Cars 'bus built in 1958 and is a diesel mechanical four wheeled vehicle similar to the successful railcars running on the Deutsche Bundesbahn. The experiment of using railbuses on BR was very shortlived as the lines tended to close down fairly rapidly making the vehicles redundant. The line opened in June 1873 and closed in November 1962.

29 July, 1960

98. An LMS class 2P 4-4-0 waits at Dalmellington to depart for Ayr; there were many of these locomotives in Ayrshire. The Dalmellington branch closed to passengers on 6 April, 1964.

9 May, 1959

99. LMS 2P No. 40695, the post grouping development of the famous Midland 2P 4-4-0, stops briefly at Dalry to load up mails for Kilmarnock. The 4.20 pm St. Enoch to Kilmarnock via Dalry travelled via Crosshouse, a fairly rare working.

29 July, 1960

100. The arrival of a special at Ardrossan Montgomerie Pier, the Caledonian terminus in town, behind a B1 4-6-0. The Caledonian Railway was always keen to poach on rival companies' territory. Through relief boat trains were diverted here in the summer when the G & SWR station was busy. The terminus closed in 1967.

10 April, 1966

101. The 'Jones Goods' on the Chain Road branch, Paisley, during the last Easter in which the locomotive was to be used to work passenger trains. In fact No. 103, the venerable first 4-6-0, was the last of the four Scottish preserved locomotives to be used on special train working on 17 October, 1965.

17 April, 1965

102. Highland Railway No. 103, the 'Jones Goods' negotiates this industrial branch line at Renfrew South on the banks of the Clyde, Easter 1965. Renfrew had no less than five stations and the Wharf branch closed on 5 June, 1967.

17 April, 1965

103. Ayr, the centre of so much activity on the 'South West'. An LMS 4F 0-6-0 is about to wheeze out to Heads of Ayr, the branch line terminus to the south, only used in the summer. Ayr station platform, down side, was unusual as it held a compound containing about forty platform weighing machines (out of sight behind loco), kept locked up, removed from various stations in the district. Further platforms were available underneath the bridge along the footpath (gas lit) while number 4 was on its own on the right hand side, confusing for passengers in a hurry perhaps!

30 July, 1960

104. The arrival of a train at Heads of Ayr with a class 5, 4-6-0. The trains ran here only in the summer to serve the nearby Butlins holiday camp which had started out as a navy training camp. The line closed in September 1968.

30 July, 1960

105. 'Caley' No. 123 scoots past Possil with the 'Scottish Rambler' in 1963 with the two preserved CR coaches in their brown and cream livery. This engine was always beautifully turned out, the buffers had thistles etched onto them and the 'spats' had thistles painted on.

12 April, 1963

106. The 5.12 pm Darvel to Kilmarnock railbus rumbles out of Newmilns. The ever expansive Caledonian Railway built a line from Strathaven towards Darvel to join up with the GSWR in 1904. The agreement between the two companies was that each Company took it in turn every six months to work the line from Strathaven to Darvel but the line did not see much traffic and closed finally in 1939. The Darvel to Kilmarnock line closed on 6 April, 1964.

19 May, 1962

107. The 'Jones Goods' on the Greenock Princes Pier
branch struggles up grade near Upper Port Glasgow,
with the Clyde and mountains of Dumbartonshire
stretching away in the background.

17th April, 1965

108. Class 4 Standard tank No. 80047 pulls away from
Ardrossan Winton Pier with the 2.48 pm to St. Enoch,
(that magnificent Victorian terminus in Glasgow now
demolished). Note the 'v' shaped route indicator on
the buffer beam.

14 November, 1968

109. No. 103 plods past Busby with a train on the East
Kilbride branch. The station buildings which were
partially destroyed by fire the previous week are
being damped by an April shower.

17 April, 1965

110. A fairly rare class in the Region was the BR Standard class 3 2-6-0 represented here by No. 77015 on the 1.41 pm Kilmarnock to Ardrossan (Town) stopper arriving at Ardrossan (South Beach). Plenty of activity here with another train due in the other direction; note the signal with arms for either way.

14 July, 1962

111. Class 4 tank No. 42194 leaves Saltcoats (Central) with the 4.20 pm Glasgow (St Enoch) to Winton Pier. No. 42194 was one of the Fairburn 2-6-4 tanks, a development of the famous Fowler 1927 design — a class totalling 645 members.

14 July, 1962

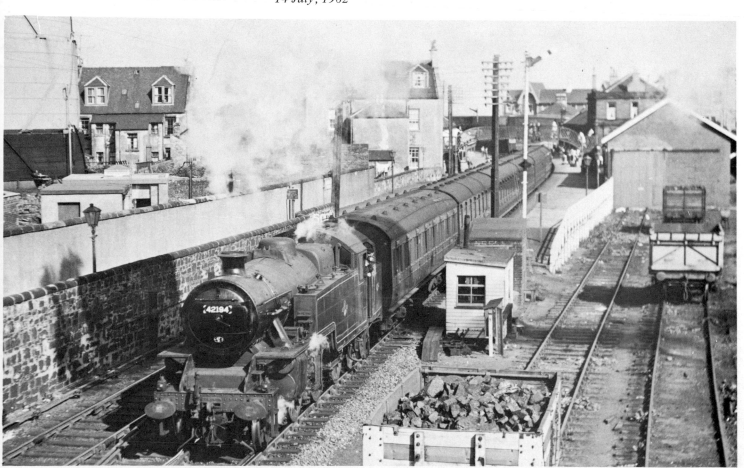

112. On the Largs branch at West Kilbride, Ayrshire with the 6.33 pm Largs to Law Junction through train hauled by a class 4 2-6-0 No. 76070. A magnificent signalbox can be seen under the footbridge, possibly the tallest signalbox in the country. Another 'South West' feature was to paint bridge numbers on instead of the usual plate. The signalbox is still there.

14 July, 1962

113. Bothwell, with a Gresley V1 2-6-2T and Gresley stock. The North British branch to Bothwell closed to passengers on 4 July, 1955 and this is the last train.

2 July, 1955

114. Strathaven, the terminus of the Caledonian branch from Hamilton. The grandiose island platform was built to handle through trains as the line was opened as a 'short road to Ayr' in 1904 as part of the Caledonian Railway scheme to run through trains to the Ayrshire coast from Lanarkshire. The line closed to Hamilton on 4 October, 1965.

2 September, 1961

115. A view through the somewhat battered crossing gates at Coalburn to the single platform terminus. Trains had to travel ½ mile up the line in order to run round, so the arrival of diesel multiple units simplified train working. A very good example of Caledonian box, signals and country station can be seen here. The crossing gates are almost miniatures owing to the narrowness of the road. The line closed on 4 October, 1965.

2 September, 1961

116. Muirkirk was the end of the line for the Caledonian Railway, the service from Lanark terminating here. The GSWR and Caledonian met there end on and the route provided a useful bypass to Glasgow for Edinburgh to Ayr trains. 'Caley' 0-6-0 No. 57295, a 2F class Drummond standard 0-6-0 goods dating in design from 1883, runs round the train from Lanark. This service was withdrawn in October 1964.

2 September, 1961

117. 'Caley' 0-6-0 No. 57618, a 3F class McIntosh 812 class of 1899, 'brews up' with an early morning train for Muirkirk at Lanark. The author having spent the night in the stock was disturbed by the movement of the train and scrambled out to photograph it before departure.

2 September, 1961

118. 'The Soldier' again at Lanark, a former Caledonian Railway station. GNSR No. 49 has backed on to the buffer stops ready for departure to Muirkirk with the BLS tour in Ayrshire. The train only ran as far as Ponfeigh on the Muirkirk line, and this was the last run of the locomotive prior to preservation in the Glasgow Museum.

16 October, 1965

119. Wilsontown, with 'Caley' 3F 0-6-0 No. 57670 on the daily goods. Wilsontown closed to passenger traffic on 10 September, 1951, but freight lasted until the 'sixties for the colliery. Note the fine Caledonian box, wooden with slate roof.

16 January, 1962

120. The signalbox at Castlehill Junction seems to be disintegrating in this picture where the train crew are assisting in a temporary reconstruction for the benefit of the photographer. The 'Caley' 0-6-0 No. 57328 has ventured onto some very rare track — the junction between the Morningside and Castlehill branches (NBR).

20 March, 1961

121. The daily goods, worked by North British N15 Class 0-6-2T No. 69196 built in 1910 to the Reid design, arrives at Peacock Cross. The Hamilton North British branch closed to passengers in September 1952 and freight in 1963. The Bothwell to Hamilton line closed to passengers in 1952 because of tunnel subsidence.

6 November, 1961

Lothian

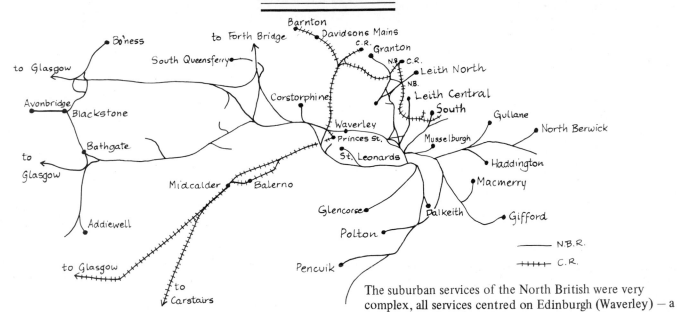

The suburban services of the North British were very complex, all services centred on Edinburgh (Waverley) — a large subterranean establishment with many bay platforms to accommodate the all-steam services from the suburbs. Dieselisation started, in the late fifties, complex workings included such sights as Gresley Pacifics on 'filling in' turns on suburban trains, a circular service and the strange contortions of lines in the Leith area, a relic of the days before the building of the Forth Bridge.

122. 'Caley' No. 123 rushes along near Midcalder with the Easter 'Scottish Rambler' for the Balerno branch. This was one of the last runs of this famous engine and coaches.

19 April, 1965

123. Colinton, on the Balerno branch, a line that was closed to regular passenger services in 1943 as an economy measure. LMS built 0-4-4 tank No. 55260 was built after the grouping in 1925 to the Caledonian design of pre-1923.

20 June, 1962

124. Class J36 0-6-0 No. 65261 shunting at Addiewell; the loco had no vacuum brake and worked mineral trains or unfitted freight only. The class was introduced on the North British in 1883 to the Holmes design and were used in France in the first world war. Addiewell was the scene of Victorian development including an industrial township built by 'Paraffin' Young in the 1870s. Oil was developed from shale and consigned by rail on the branch.

30 October, 1960

125. Class J35 No. 64468 and Gresley stock about to leave Bathgate on a Hyndland local. Bathgate, once an important junction with branch trains to Morningside, Coatbridge, and Blackstone, closed in May 1930. Services to Airdrie and Edinburgh were withdrawn in January 1956.

31 December, 1955

126. Avonbridge, with Class J36 No. 65281 on the daily goods; passenger services were withdrawn in May 1930.

26 December, 1960

127. North British No. 64603 of J37 class at South
Queensferry. The South Queensferry branch ceased
to be of importance after the construction of the
Forth Bridge in 1890 but passenger services lasted
until 1929 and freight until 1967.

13 April, 1963

128. Granton Harbour, with North British 4-4-2T No.
67492, class C16 of 1915, hauling an SLS railtour
about to traverse the Duke of Buccleuch line. The
line was promoted by the Duke of Buccleuch as a
mineral railway in 1857 and sold out to the
Caledonian Railway. A portion at Granton Square
remained in his ownership until acquired by the
Forth Ports Authority in 1962.

6 September, 1958

129. No. 64947 of class J39, the LNER development of the North Eastern 0-6-0, shunting in the one time passenger station at Leith (Citadel). The line was closed to passengers in April 1952.

4 March, 1960

130. A fine view of the Gresley 3 cylinder V1 class 2-6-2 tank, introduced in 1930 for express suburban work, at Bonnington hauling a van train from Leith (Citadel).

4 August, 1959

131. Class 2 2-6-0 No. 78046 makes short work of a light load of two Caledonian coaches en route for the Balerno branch near Slateford with a special at Easter 1965.

19 April, 1965

132. Corstorphine, the terminus of the short suburban branch line in Edinburgh — a useful place to put an A3 class out of the way of busy Waverley station. The loco is Pacific No. 60060 *The Tetrarch* with double chimney. The line closed in January 1968.

15 June, 1963

133. The St. Leonards branch goods with NB class J35 0-6-0 No. 64486 working a winter mixed freight with coal and general merchandise through the rocks round the back of Arthur's Seat to the old Edinburgh and Dalkeith Railway terminus. This line closed completely on 5 August, 1968.

19 October, 1955

134. Davidson's Mains with 'Caley' 0-6-0 No. 57654 shunting the daily goods. The Barnton 'Caley' branch closed to passengers on 7 May, 1951.

22 March, 1960

135. Another of the short suburban branches from Edinburgh with V1 2-6-2T ready to leave Musselburgh on a train for Edinburgh (Waverley). Notice the overall roof and raised lettering on station name-board, painted regional light blue. The line closed 7 September, 1964.

29 May, 1958

136. Gullane, with the North British J35 0-6-0 of 1908 running round its train on the occasion of an SLS special. The LNER post war stock with roof board slots was most comfortable to ride in. Gullane closed to passengers in September 1932.

11 June, 1960

137. Class V1 2-6-2 No. 67659 stands at North Berwick with a pre-dieselisation train of Gresley stock. This former North British branch line still survives, one of the few on the system that have not been closed. Notice the scissors crossover (utilised for engine release) on a sharp bend, quite a feat in track work.

1 May, 1954

138. Haddington, with a NB 0-6-0 tender first on a week's tour special, 11 June, 1960. What a fabulous lamp! The lamp is mounted on a wooden post with rungs for the staff to climb up every night to light the gas. Round the foot of the column are rail ramps for re-railing derailed wagons. The line closed to passengers on 5 December, 1949.

139. No. 64479 of J35 class (1908) shunts the daily goods at Dalkeith on what was originally the Edinburgh and Dalkeith Railway opened in 1831 to the Scottish standard gauge of 4ft 6in and worked by horse traction. The Edinburgh terminus was at St. Leonards, Waverley not being in existence at that time. Dalkeith closed to passengers in January 1942.
21 April, 1960

140. An engine and brake van at Polton, which closed on 10 September 1951. The locomotive is a Class J36 0-6-0 of Holmes design of 1888. Notice the superb North British valancing on the station roof.
20 May, 1960

141. The Humbie branch goods arrives at Pencaitland
with Class 2 2-6-0 No. 46462. The Gifford branch
was opened as a light railway in 1901 and worked by
the North British Railway. Gifford closed to freight
in 1948 and Humbie in 1960.

4 March, 1960

142. Lasswade Viaduct, with the Polton Goods crossing with class J35 0-6-0 No. 64479, a Reid NB design of 1908. Polton to Esk Valley Junction closed to passengers on 10 September 1951.

20 April, 1960

143. Ormiston, the junction station for the lines to Macmerry and Gifford. The Gifford branch was closed to passengers in 1933 but freight continued until 1948 between Gifford and Humbie. Class 2 2-6-0 pauses with a freight train.

4 March, 1960

Borders

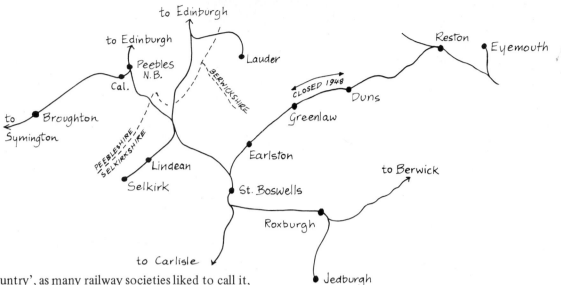

'The Scott country', as many railway societies liked to call it, was the area between the Scottish Region main lines and the North Eastern Region cross border lines. In pre-grouping times some of the lines were actually partly North British and partly North Eastern. The main line of importance was the Waverley line, the longest main line in Scotland that, like the Great Central and Somerset & Dorset, has now sunk into oblivion. The closure of the Waverley line from Edinburgh to Carlisle was much more of a disaster than closure of comparable English main lines. An attempt was made briefly to finance the line by public money but the scheme was launched too late and by 6 January 1969 Britain's most sorrowful closure took place. The Borders' branch lines fed into the Waverley but they passed through sparsely populated countryside with little traffic.

144. The last train to Lauder on what was once the Lauder Light Railway, plods up the bank out of Fountainhall Junction. No. 78049, a Standard Class 2 2-6-0, makes heavy work of a two coach special. Some of the passengers were lucky enough to be treated to a mammoth 'bun fight' organised by Lauder Council when the train eventually arrived at the end of the branch. The line was well known for its tender-tank locomotives (J69 0-6-0T with tender) which ran as such to reduce the weight on this line, being lightly laid with sharp curves.

15 November, 1958

145. The Peebles branch with North British J37 class No. 64614 working a rail recovery train between Peebles (West) and Peebles (East). Peebles (West) to Symington closed to passengers in June 1950 but freight still ran from Peebles (East) connecting the North British with the Caledonian after closure. Note the fine distant signal. Peebles (West) to Peebles Junction closed on 1 August, 1959.

14 November, 1961

146. No. 55124, a McIntosh Caledonian Railway 0-4-4 tank of 1895 shunts the empty stock of the B.L.S. Pentlands & Tinto railtour at Broughton, the then terminus of the freight only line from Symington, which closed finally on 4 April, 1966.

22 May, 1961

147. Jedburgh, with B1 class 4-6-0 No. 61324 departing on an Easter 'Scottish Rambler' railtour to Roxburgh. The line was closed to passenger traffic in August 1948 following floods in the Border areas during that year.

14 April, 1963

148. The nameboards at St. Boswells on the Waverley route indicate the changing fortune of the branch lines in the area. Jedburgh, closed in August 1948, has had 'bus service' added on after its name. The line to Berwick closed on 15 June, 1964.

22 May, 1961

149. Duns, the terminus of the branch from Reston with the 'Scottish Rambler' at Easter 1963. The line was once a through route to St. Boswells but the section from Duns to Greenlaw was washed away in the great floods of August 1948. The Duns to Reston section closed to passengers in 1951.

14 April, 1963

150. The 'Scottish Rambler' again with B1 class 4-6-0 No. 61324 on the Greenlaw branch at Earlston from which section passenger traffic was withdrawn in August 1948 as a result of flooding.

14 April, 1963

151. Eyemouth, in a sea mist with class J39 0-6-0 No. 64917 on the morning train to Berwick. The line was closed in August 1948 when floods washed away a viaduct. The damage took 10 months to repair but in spite of the high costs involved the line closed completely in 1962.

6 September, 1958

152. *Wandering Willie* caught 'not wandering' in the sidings at Hawick. The North British 'Scott' class were introduced in 1912 and named after characters from the Scott novels. *Wandering Willie* had the dubious honour of being sandwiched in between 62439 *Father Ambrose* and 62441 *Black Duncan*. The 'Scott' class worked branch lines and suburban trains throughout the NB system.

7 September, 1958

153. Lindean, the last station before Selkirk with a special worked by North British 'Glen' class No. 62471 *Glen Falloch* built in 1913. Selkirk closed for freight traffic in 1964.

4 April, 1959

154. Selkirk station showing the substantial stone frontage, with buildings used for public and residential purposes. The line closed to passengers on 10 September, 1951. Selkirk station still sold passenger tickets after the service had been withdrawn but for journeys from Galashiels.

4 April, 1959

Dumfries & Galloway

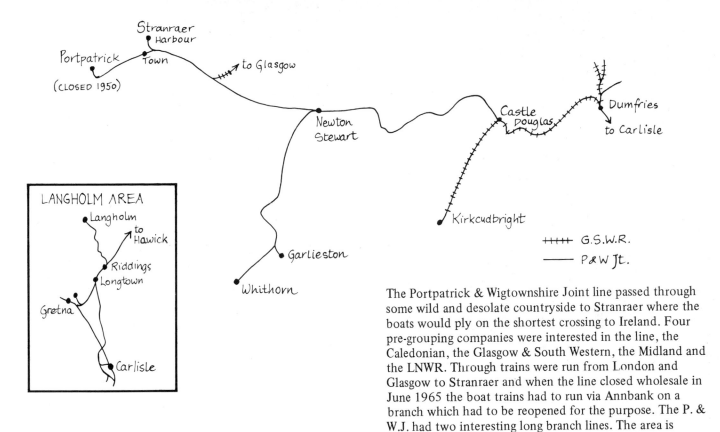

LANGHOLM AREA

Stranraer Harbour
Portpatrick (CLOSED 1950)
Town
to Glasgow
Newton Stewart
Garlieston
Whithorn
Castle Douglas
Dumfries
to Carlisle
Kirkcudbright

Langholm
to Hawick
Riddings
Longtown
Gretna
Carlisle

++++ G.S.W.R.
——— P&W Jt.

The Portpatrick & Wigtownshire Joint line passed through some wild and desolate countryside to Stranraer where the boats would ply on the shortest crossing to Ireland. Four pre-grouping companies were interested in the line, the Caledonian, the Glasgow & South Western, the Midland and the LNWR. Through trains were run from London and Glasgow to Stranraer and when the line closed wholesale in June 1965 the boat trains had to run via Annbank on a branch which had to be reopened for the purpose. The P. & W.J. had two interesting long branch lines. The area is devoid of any railways now, in fact a large part of south west Scotland is completely railless.

155. Langholm in a 'Scotch mist' with Class J39 0-6-0 No. 64912 of Carlisle Canal shed. The engine shed still survives in this picture of the branch train although the shed track has been removed. This line closed on 15 June, 1964.
15 November, 1958

156. The morning passenger train about to leave Kirkcudbright for Dumfries behind a Stanier class 3 2-6-2T. After spending the night in the cells of the local police station the author was able to photograph the first train of the day. The Kirkcudbright Railway was opened in February 1864, the line closed to passengers in May 1965.

30 July, 1960

157. The remains of the passenger station at Garlieston, once used by passengers detraining for the harbour. The Whithorn goods used to run three days a week with a conditional working down the short Garlieston branch which was closed to passenger traffic in 1903. Garlieston was used by boat trains taking people to the Isle of Man on day trips until the 1930s.

30 May, 1965

158. The Whithorn goods arrives at Newton Stewart with a 'Caley' 0-6-0 No. 57340. The line closed to freight traffic on 5 October, 1964.

1 August, 1960

159. Caledonian 0-6-0 No. 57661 shunts some conflats with BD containers at Dumfries Caledonian station, terminus of the former Caledonian branch from Lockerbie, closed to passengers in May 1952 and to freight, April 1966.

15 April, 1963

160. The Portpatrick & Wigtownshire Joint line had a very lengthy branch from Newton Stewart to Whithorn. During the winter of 1964 the track was lifted and sold or used elsewhere. The scene here is at Wigtown, the first station on the branch, and the rails are being cut up on the spot.

30 May, 1965

161. The remains of Millisle Junction with the Garlieston branch leading off to the right and track being lifted.

30 May, 1965

162. The Whithorn goods stops at Whauphill with the thrice weekly goods from Newton Stewart behind 'Caley' 0-6-0 No. 57340. The passenger service had ceased in September 1950.

1 August, 1960

163. A rare photograph of 'Caley' 0-4-4 tank No. 55232 built in 1915, at Moffat, a branch which left the Carlisle to Glasgow main line at Beattock, Dumfriesshire. This line closed in December 1954. The Moffat branch was worked by an 0-4-4T as shown, the loco worked 'push and pull' although not fitted as such.

4 December, 1954

Line	Former Company		Date Closed
Aberfeldy – Ballinluig	High	P	3.5.65@
		F	1.3.65
Aberfoyle – Kirkintilloch	NB	P	1.10.51
Aberfoyle – Campsie Glen (Lennox Castle Sdg)		F	5.10.59@
Lennox Castle Sdg – Lennoxtown		F	28.9.64@
Lennoxtown – Kirkintilloch		F	4.4.66@
Airdrie – Bathgate Upper – Edinburgh (Bathgate Jn).	NB	P	9.1.56
(Summer Seasonal service over this route retained until 1960)			
Airdrie – Whifflet Upper	Cal	P	3.5.43
Airdrie East – Calder (Imperial Tube Works)		F	6.7.64@
Alford – Kintore	GNS	P	2.1.50
Alford – Kintore (Paradise Sdg)		F	3.1.66@
Paradise Siding – Kintore		F	7.11.66@
Alloa (Kincardine Jn) – Culross – Dunfermline	NB	P	7.7.30
(Kincardine/Valleyfield Colliery had closed to through traffic but reopened 2.5.60)			
Alloa (West Jn) – Larbert (Alloa Jn)	Cal	P	29.1.68
Alloa West Jn – Longcarse Jn (excl)		F	18.5.70@
Longcarse Jn (excl) – Throsk		F	6.5.68@
Throsk – Alloa Jn.		F	1.4.78
Alva – Cambus	NB	P	1.11.54
Alva – Menstrie		F	2.3.64@
Alyth Junction – Dundee West (Ninewells Jn)	Cal	P	10.1.55
Newtyle Goods – Alyth Junction		F	7.9.64@
Newtyle Jn – Auchterhouse		F	5.5.58@
Auchterhouse – Fairmuir Jn		F	25.1.65@
Fairmuir Jn – Ninewells Jn		F	6.11.67@
Alyth Town – Alyth Junction	Cal	P	2.7.51
		F	1.3.65
Annan Shawhill – Kirtlebridge	Cal	P	27.4.31
		F	?
Annbank – Mauchline	GSW	P	4.1.43
(Except Summer Seasonal services. Reopened 14.6.65 on closure of Dumfries/Stranraer line, but closed again 5.5.75)			
Arbroath (St Vigean's Jn) – Forfar (Guthrie Jn)	Cal	P	5.12.55
St. Vigean's Jn – Letham Mill L.C.		F	5.12.55@
Letham Mill L.C. – Colliston		F	1.1.59@
Colliston – Guthrie Jn		F	25.1.65@
Ardrossan: Castlehill Jn – Parkhouse Jn	GSW	P	1.1.68
		F	30.9.69@
Ardrossan North – Uplawmoor	Cal	P	4.7.32
(Line retained for Boat Trains, diverted via GSW 1947)			
Ardrossan Montgomerie Pier–Stevenston No 1	Cal/LMS	All	6.5.68@
Stevenston (new connect.) – Kilwinning E.	Cal	All	1947
Kilwinning East – Giffen (excl)		F	30.3.53@
Giffen (excl) – Lugton East Jn		F	31.5.50@
Lugton Jn (GBK) – Uplawmoor			14.12.64@
Balerno – Edinburgh (Balerno Jn)	Cal	P	1.11.43
(Temporary closure ... officially closed 13.6.49)			
Balerno Goods – Balerno Jn		F	4.12.67@
Balerno – Ravelrig Jn		P	11.9.39
Balerno Goods g.f. – Ravelrig Jn		F	9.9.63@
Ballachulish (Glencoe) – Connel Ferry	Cal	P	28.3.66@
		F	14.6.65
Ballater – Aberdeen (Ferryhill Jn)	GNS	P	28.2.66
Ballater – Culter		F	18.7.66@
Culter – Ferryhill Jn		F	2.1.67@
Balloch (Forth & Clyde Jn) – Stirling	NB	P	1.10.34
(Excludes Gartness Jn/Buchlyvie, served by Aberfoyle trains)			
Forth & Clyde Jn – Croftengea Siding		F	9.4.65@
Croftengea Siding – Jamestown		F	1.9.64@
Jamestown – Drymen		F	5.10.59@
Drymen – Gartness Jn		F	1.11.50
Buchlyvie – Mye Siding		F	?
Mye Siding – Port of Monteith		F	1.12.52@
Port of Monteith – Stirling		F	5.10.59@
Balquhidder – Comrie	Cal	P	1.10.51@
		F	25.9.50
Banavie Pier – Fort William (Banavie Jn)	NB	P	4.9.39
		F	6.8.51
Banff – Tillynaught	GNS	P	6.7.64
		F	6.5.68@
Bankfoot – Strathord	Cal	P	13.4.31
		F	7.9.64@
Barassie – Kilmarnock	GSW	P	3.3.69
(Reopened 5.5.75 on closure of Ayr/Annbank/Mauchline line)			
Barnton – Craigleith	Cal	P	7.5.51
Barnton – Davidson's Mains		F	7.5.51@
Davidson's Mains – Craigleith		F	1.6.60@
Beith Town – Lugton	GBK	P	5.11.62
Beith Town – Barrmill Jn		F	5.10.64@
Blackston Junction – Bathgate Upper	NB	P	1.5.30
Blackston Junction – Westfield Paper Mill		F	28.12.64@
Westfield Paper Mill – Bathgate Lower		F	1.5.67@
Bathgate Lower – Bathgate Upper		F	3.9.73@
Blackwood Jn – Tillietudlum (Southfield Jn)	Cal	P	1.10.51
		F	4.1.60@
Blairgowrie – Coupar Angus	Cal	P	10.1.55
		F	6.12.65@
Boat of Garten – Craigellachie	GNS	P	18.10.65
Boat of Garten – Aberlour		F	4.11.68@
Aberlour – Craigellachie		F	15.11.71@
Boddam – Ellon	GNS	P	31.10.32
		F	31.12.48@
Bo'ness – Polmont (Bo'ness Jn)	NB	P	7.5.56
Bo'ness – Kinneil Colliery		F	19.7.65@
Bonnybridge – Greenhill	Cal	P	28.7.30
Bonnybridge Canal – Greenhill		F	7.12.64@
Bothwell – Blairhill & Gartsherrie (Sunnyside Jn)	NB	P	10.9.51
Bothwell Jn – Bellshill – Whifflet East		F	? @
Bothwell – Fallside (Bothwell Jn)	Cal	All	5.6.50@
Bothwell – Shettleston	NB	P	4.7.55
Bothwell – Mount Vernon North		F	6.6.61@
Mount Vernon North – Shettleston (Argosy Sdg)		F	4.10.65@
Brechin – Bridge of Dun	Cal	P	4.8.52
Brechin – Forfar (South Jn)	Cal	P	4.8.52
Brechin – Careston		F	17.3.58@
Careston – Justinhaugh		F	7.9.64@
Justinhaugh – Forfar South Jn		F	4.9.67@
Bridge of Earn – Ladybank	NB	P	19.9.55
(Reopened for through Edinburgh/Perth services 6.10.75)			
Bridgeton Cross – Carmyle – Newton	Cal	P	5.10.64
Bridgeton Cross – Tollcross		All	5.10.64@
Tollcross – Tollcross East		F	4.4.66@
Brocketsbrae – Hamilton (Ferniegair Jn)	Cal	P	1.10.51
Brocketsbrae – Tillietudlum (Southfield Jn)	F		21.9.53@
Southfield Jn – Dalserf Jn		F	4.1.60@
Dalserf Jn – Ferniegair Jn		F	20.4.64@
Callander – Dunblane	Cal	P	1.11.65@
		F	7.6.65
Campbeltown – Macrihanish	CMLR	All	Nov. 31@
Carmyllie – Elliot Junction	D&A	P	2.12.29
Carmyllie – Elliot (Metal Box Co's Sdg)		F	24.5.65@
Catrine – Mauchline (Brackenhill Jn)	GSW	P	3.5.43
		F	6.7.64@
Charlestown – Dunfermline (Elbowend Jn)	NB	P	1.11.26
Charlestown – Crombie RNAD Sdg		F	24.2.64@
Clydebank East – Yoker (Clydebank East Jn)	NB	All	14.9.59@
Coalburn – Hamilton (Haughhead Jn)	Cal	P	4.10.65
Coalburn – Auchlochan Colliery			4.10.65@
Auchlochan Colliery – Larkhall Central		F	19.8.68@
Larkhall Central – Haughhead Jn		F	4.11.68@
Coatbridge Central – Rutherglen (Jn)	Cal	P	7.11.66
(Reopened 1.5.72 for Glasgow Cen/Perth service until 4.5.74 incl.)			
Comrie – Crieff – Gleneagles	Cal	P	6.7.64
Comrie – Crieff		F	15.6.64
			6.7.64@
Crieff – Muthill		F	2.11.64@
Muthill – Gleneagles		F	1.9.64@
Corstorphine – Edinburgh (Haymarket West Jn)	NB	P	1.1.68
		F	5.2.68@
Crianlarich (Jn East) – Callander	Cal	P	1.11.65
Crianlarich Lower – Callander		All	28.9.65@
(Due to landslide in Glenogle a bus service operated in lieu from 28th September 1965 until actual date of closure)			

Route	Company	Type	Date
Crieff – Perth (Almond Valley Jn)	Cal	P	1.10.51
Crieff – Perth (Dewar's Sdg)		F	11.9.67@
Cronberry – Auchinleck	GSW	P	3.7.50
		F	6.12.76@
Dalkeith – Millerhill (Glenesk Jn)	NB	P	5.1.42
		F	10.8.64@
Dalmellington – Ayr (Dalrymple Jn)	GSW	P	6.4.64
Dalmellington – Waterside		F	6.7.64@
Dalmeny Jn – Winchburgh Jn	NB	P	1.1.73
Dalry – Kilmarnock	GSW	P	18.4.66
(Through passenger services continued until ...		All	1.10.73@
Darvel – Strathaven Central	GSW/Cal	All	11.9.39
Darvel – Kilmarnock (Hurlford Jn)	GSW	P	6.4.64
Darvel – Hurlford (Mayfield Sdg)		F	6.7.64@
Hurlford: Mayfield Sdg – Mineral Sdgs		F	20.9.65@
Hurlford Mineral Sdgs – Hurlford Jn		F	24.1.66@
Denny – Larbert (Bonnywater Jn)	Cal	P	28.7.30
Denny – Bonnybridge SSEB		F	4.10.71@
Bonnybridge SSEB – Larbert Jn		F	3.4.72@
Denny West Jn – Carmuirs West Jn		F	20.7.65@
Dolphinton – Carstairs (Dolphinton Jn)	Cal	P	4.6.45
		F	1.11.50@
Dornoch – The Mound	High	All	13.6.60@
Douglas West (Poniel Jn) – Brocketsbrae	Cal	P	11.9.39
(Alton Heights/Brocketsbrae used by one SO train until 2.5.42)			
Poniel Jn – Alton Heights (excl)		F	13.9.54@
Alton Heights (excl) – Brocketsbrae		F	21.9.53@
Dumbarton (Dunglass Jn) – Rutherglen	Cal	P	5.10.64
Dunglass Jn – Old Kirkpatrick		F	5.10.64@
Kilbowie – Yoker Ferry		F	11.10.76@
Partick Central – Strathclyde Jn		All	5.10.64@
(Stobcross/Strathclyde Jn/Rutherglen due to reopen P May 1979)			
Dumbarton (East Jn) – Bowling (Dunglass Jn)	NB	All	25.4.60
Dumfries – Lockerbie	Cal	P	19.5.52
		F	18.4.66@
Dundee East – Camperdown Jn	D&A	P	5.1.59
Dundee West – Buckingham Jn	Cal	P	3.5.65
Dumfermline: Townhill Jn – Touch North Jn	NB	P	6.5.68
Duns – Reston	NB	P	10.9.51
		F	7.11.66@
East Kilbride – Hamilton (Hunthill Jn)	Cal	P	14.7.24
(Previously Closed 1.10.14 – 1.10.23)			
Mavor & Coulson's Sgd – Hunthill Jn		F	18.11.35
Mavor & Coulson's Sgd – East Kilbride		F	24.1.66@
(Special workings continued until outbreak of 1939/45 war.)			
Edinburgh: Abbeyhill Jn – Piershill Jn Loop	NB	P	7.9.64
Edinburgh: Haymarket West Jn – Dalry Jn	Cal	P	2.3.64
		F	9.3.64@
Edinburgh (Portobello East Jn) – Hawick – – Carlisle (Port Carlisle Jn)	NB	P	6.1.69
Millerhill Jn – Butlerfield NCB		F	28.6.72@
Butlerfield NCB – Lady Victoria Pit		F	20.12.71@
Gorebridge (Lady Victoria Pit) – Hawick		F	28.4.69@
Hawick – Longtown		All	6.1.69@
Longtown – Brunthill		F	31.8.70@
Stainton Jn – Canal Jn		F	4.8.69@
Canal Jn – Port Carlisle Jn		All	6.1.69@
Edinburgh Princes Street – Slateford Jn	Cal	P	6.9.65
		F	15.8.66@
Edzell – Brechin	Cal	P	27.4.31
		F	7.9.64@
(Passenger service reopened 4.7.38, experimentally, closed again 26.9.38)			
Elderslie (Cart Jn) – Dalry (Brownhill Jn)	GSW	P	27.6.66
Cart Jn – Kilbirnie		F	3.7.72@
Kilbirnie – Brownhill Jn		F	77@
Elgin – Buckie – Cairnie Junction	GNS	P	6.5.68@
Elgin East – Lossie Jn		F	28.3.66
Lossie Jn – Buckie		F	20.4.64
Buckie – Cairnie Jn		All	6.5.68
Elgin – Craigellachie – Keith Junction	GNS	P	6.5.68
Elgin East – Craigellachie		F	4.11.68@
Craigellachie – Dufftown		F	15.11.71@
Eyemouth – Burnmouth	NB	All	5.2.62@
Fairlie Pier – Fairlie Pier Jn	GSW	P	1.10.71
(Temporary closure ... officially closed 31.7.72)			
Fochabers Town – Orbliston Junction	High	P	14.9.31
		F	28.3.66@
Forfar (North Jn) – Dundee East (Broughty Jn)	Cal	P	10.1.55
Forfar North Jn – Kingsmuir		F	8.12.58@
Kingsmuir – Broughty Jn		F	9.10.67@
Forres – Aviemore	High	P	18.10.65
Forres West Jn – Forres South Jn			15.8.66@
Forres South Jn – Dallas Dhu Siding		F	21.5.67@
Dallas Dhu Siding – Boat of Garten		F	6.9.65
			18.10.65@
Boat of Garten – Aviemore North		F	4.11.68@
Forres East Jn – Forres South Jn	High	P	18.10.65
		F	21.5.67@
Fort Augustus – Spean Bridge	NB	P	1.12.33
		F	1.1.47@
Fort George – Gollanfield Junction	High	P	5.4.43
		F	11.8.58@
Fortrose – Muir of Ord	High	P	1.10.51
		F	13.6.60@
Fraserburgh – Aberdeen (Dyce Jn)	GNS	P	4.10.65
Gartcosh Jn – Gartsherrie South Jn		P	5.11.62
(Reopened 3.5.76, on diversion of London/Fort William services)			
Gifford – Edinburgh (Monktonhall Jn)	NB	P	3.4.33
Gifford – Humbie		F	8.48@
Humbie – Saltoun		F	2.5.60@
Saltoun – Smeaton		F	24.5.65@
Glasgow Buchanan Street – Sighthill East Jn	Cal	P	7.11.66@
Glasgow St Enoch (Gorbals Jn) – Strathbungo Jn	GBK	P	18.4.66
		F	23.6.73@
Glasgow St Enoch – Shields Jn	GSW	P	27.6.66
Glasgow St Enoch – Clyde Jn		R	5.6.67@
Glencorse – Millerhill	NB	P	1.5.33
Glencorse (Penicuik Gas Works) – Roslin		F	1.7.59@
Roslin – Bilston Glen Colliery		F	1.6.69@
Grange – Grange North Jn	GNS	All	7.3.60@
Grangemouth – Falkirk Grahamston	Cal	P	29.1.68
(Grangemouth Jn)			
Granton – Powderhall (Bonnington South Jn)	NB	P	2.11.25
Greenock Princes Pier – Kilmacolm	GSW	P	2.2.59
(Retained for Ocean Liner Boat trains until 14.2.66)			
Greenock Princes Pier – Kilmacolm		F	26.9.66@
(Greenock CPA Terminal – Cartsburn Jn reopened F 7.6.71)			
Gullane – Longniddry (Aberlady Jn)	NB	P	12.9.32
		F	15.6.64@
Haddington – Longniddry	NB	P	5.12.49
		F	1.4.68@
Hamilton – Bothwell	NB	P	15.9.52
Hamilton – Peacock Cross (Allanshaw Foundry)		All	15.9.52@
Allanshaw Foundry – Blantyre Jn		F	11.2.63@
Blantyre Jn – Bothwell		All	15.9.52@
Heads of Ayr (Butlin's Camp) – Ayr	GSW	P	16.9.68@
(Alloway Jn)		F	7.12.59
High Blantyre (Auchenraith Jn) – Blantyre Jn	Cal	P	1.10.45
		F	by 1958@
Holehouse Jn – Rankinston – Belston Jn	GSW	P	3.4.50
Holehouse Jn – Littlemill Colliery		?	@
Littlemill Colliery – Belston Jn		F	1.1.75@
Hopeman – Alves	High	P	14.9.31
Hopeman – Burghead		F	30.12.57@
Hyndland – Partick Jn	NB	P	5.11.60
		F	5.5.58
(Retained to serve Hyndland EMU Maintenance Depot)			
Inverbervie – Montrose (Broomfield Jn)	NB	P	1.10.51
		F	23.5.66@
Irvine Bank Street – Kilwinning	Cal	P	28.7.30
		F	1.6.39@
Irvine (Byrehill Jn) – Stevenston (Dubbs Jn)	GSW	P	6.4.64
Irvine – Crosshouse	GSW	P	6.4.64
Irvine Goods – Crosshouse		F	11.10.65@
Jedburgh – Roxburgh	NB	P	13.8.48
		F	10.8.64@
Kelso – St Boswells (Kelso Jn)	NB	P	15.6.64
		F	1.4.68@
Kelso – Tweedmouth	NE	P	15.6.64
		F	29.3.65@
Kilbirnie South – Giffen	Cal	P	1.12.30
Glengarnock High – Giffen		F	1.12.30@

Killin – Killin Junction	Cal	P	1.11.65
		F	2.11.64

Actual, including access to Loch Tay loco shed 28.9.65@
(Due to landslide in Glenogle a bus service operated in Lieu from 28th September 1965 until acutal date of closure.)

Kilsyth – Kirkintilloch (Kelvin Valley West Jn) NB		P	6.8.51
Kilsyth – Twechar		F	4.5.64@
Twechar – Kelvin Valley West Jn		F	4.4.66
Kilsyth (Kelvin Valley East Jn) – Maryhill	NB	P	2.4.51
Kelvin Valley East Jn – Torrance		F	6.56@
Torrance – Balmore		F	5.10.59@
Balmore – Maryhill Park East Jn		F	31.7.61@
Kinross Junction – Alloa	NB	P	15.6.64
Kinross Junction – Dollar		F	20.4.64
			15.6.64@
Dollar – Alloa (Co-op Coal Siding)		F	25.6.73@
Kirkcudbright – Castle Douglas	GSW	P	3.5.65
		F	14.6.65@
Kirkhill (Kirkhill Jn) – Carmyle (Westburn Jn) Cal		P	17.6.57
		F	1.8.66@
Kirkintilloch – Lenzie Junction	NB	P	7.9.64
		F	4.4.66@
Kirriemuir – Forfar (Kirriemuir Jn)	Cal	P	4.8.52
		F	21.6.65@
Ladybank – Mawcarse Junction	NB	P	5.6.50
Ladybank – Auchtermuchty		F	29.1.57@
Auchtermuchty – Mawcarse Junction		F	5.10.64@
Lanark – Carstairs (Lanark Jn South Curve)	Cal	P	18.4.66
		F	7.10.68@
Langholm – Riddings Junction	NB	P	15.6.64
		F	18.9.67@
Larbert (Larbert Jn) – Kilsyth	K&B	P	1.2.35
Bonnywater Jn – Dennyloadhead		All	1.2.35@
Dennyloanhead – Banknock		F	1.3.56@
Banknock – Kilsyth		F	4.5.64@
Lauder – Fountainhall Junction	NB	P	12.9.32
		F	1.10.58@
Leadburn – Dolphinton	NB	All	1.4.33

(Leadburn/Macbie Hill reopened F during 1939/45 war, closed 12.60)

Leith Central – Abbeyhill/Piershill	NB	P	7.4.52

(Retained as DMU servicing depot until ... 1.5.72@

Leith North–Edinburgh Princes St (Dalry Mid Jn) Cal		P	30.4.62
Leith North – George Street Depot		F	5.8.68@
George Street Depot – Newhaven Jn		F	28.2.68@
Newhaven Jn – Coltfield Jn		F	4.9.67@
Coltfield Jn – Dalry Middle Jn – Dalry Jn		F	9.3.64@
Leslie – Markinch	NB	P	4.1.32
Leslie – Auchmuty Jn		F	9.10.67@
Leuchars Junction – St Andrews	NB	P	6.1.69@
Leuchars Junction – Guard Bridge		All	6.1.69@
Guard Bridge – St Andrews		F	20.6.66
Leven – Thorton Junction	NB	P	6.10.69
Leven – East of Fife Central Jn		F	18.7.66
			6.10.69@
Loch Tay – Killin	Cal	All	11.9.39

(Retained for access to loco shed until ... 28.9.65@

Lochty – East of Fife Central Jn	NB	F	10.8.64@
Lossiemouth – Elgin (Lossie Jn)	GNS	P	4.6.64
		F	28.3.66@
Lybster – Wick	High	All	3.4.44

(Temporary closure from this date, actual 1.2.51)

Macduff – Inveramsay	GNS	P	1.10.51
Macduff – Turriff		F	1.8.61@
Turriff – Inveramsay		F	3.1.66@
Macmerry – Ormiston	NB	P	1.7.25
		F	2.5.60@
Manuel Low Level – Bo'ness Low Jn	NB	P	1.5.33
		F	? @
Manuel Low Level – Coatbridge (Greenside Jn) NB		P	1.5.30
Manuel Low Level – Causewayend		F	? @
Causewayend – Bowhouse		F	6.7.64@
Bowhouse – Blackston Junction		F	c 1960@
Blackston Junction – Avonbridge		F	28.12.64@
Avonbridge – Slamannan		F	c 1940@
Slamannan – Rawyards		F	1.9.49@

Rawyards – Commonhead		F	1.5.56@
Commonhead – Kipps Incline Foot		F	6.7.64@
Kipps Incline Foot – Greenside Jn		F	18.8.71@
Maryhill Central – Stobcross (Via Kelvinbridge)	Cal	P	2.11.59
Maryhill Central Jn – Kelvinbridge		F	6.7.64@
Kelvinbridge – Stobcross Jn		F	14.8.60@
Methil – Thornton Junction	NB	P	10.1.55
Thornton Junction – West Wemyss		F	2.12.63@
West Wemyss – Lochhead Colliery		F	? @
Lochhead Colliery – Methil West		F	15.10.66@
Methven – Methven Junction	Cal	P	27.9.37
Methven Town – Methven Junction		F	25.1.65@
Moffat – Beattock	Cal	P	6.12.54
		F	6.4.64@
Moniaive – Dumfries (Cairn Valley Jn)	GSW	P	3.5.43
		F	4.7.49@
Montrose – Broomfield Jn	Cal	P	30.4.34
Montrose East – Broomfield Jn		F	19.6.67@
Montrose – Broomfield Jn – Dubton Jn	NB/Cal	P	4.8.52
Montrose – Broomfield Jn	NB	F	19.6.67@
Broomfield Jn – Dubton Junction	Cal	F	20.6.63@
Morningside – Bathgate (Polkemmet Jn)	NB	P	1.5.30
Morningside – Castlehill Jn		F	15.7.74@
Castlehill Jn – Fauldhouse & Crofthead		F	? @
Fauldhouse & Crofthead – Whitrigg Colliery		F	2.5.66@
Whitrigg Colliery – Polkemmet Jn		F	20.1.69@
Morningside – Holytown (Cleland Jn)	Cal	P	1.12.30
Morningside – Newmains		F	5.2.51@
Newmains – Cleland Jn		F	c 1930s@
Muirkirk – Ayr (Hawkhill Jn)	GSW	P	10.9.51
Muirkirk – Cronberry (excl)		F	10.2.69@
Cronberry – Dykes Jn		F	7.3.64@
Dykes Jn – Belston Jn		F	3.4.66@
Belston Jn – Drongan		F	1.1.75@
Blackhouse Jn/Hawkhill Jn		All	5.5.75@

(Except Summer Seasonal services Annbank/Ayr. Reopened P 14.6.65 between Annbank and Hawkhill Jn on closure of Dumfries/Stranraer line, but closed again 5.5.75)

Muirkirk – Lanark (Smyllum West Jn)	Cal	P	5.10.64
Muirkirk – Ponfeigh		All	5.10.64@
Ponfeigh – Lanark Racecourse – Smyllum East Jn F			15.1.68@
Lanark Racecourse – Smyllum West Jn		F	18.10.65@
Musselburgh – Joppa (Newhailes Jn)	NB	P	7.9.64
		F	6.9.71@
Newburgh (Glenburnie Jn) – St Fort	NB	P	12.2.51
Glenburnie Jn – Lindores		F	4.4.60@
Lindores – St Fort		F	5.10.64@
Newhouse – Airdrie	Cal	P	1.12.30
Newhouse – Chapelhall		F	4.4.66@
Chapelhall – Calderbank		F	c 1939@
Calderbank – Airdrie		F	31.7.41@
Newport-on-Tay East – Dundee (Tay Bridge South)	NB	P	5.5.69@
		F	2.1.67
North Leith – Abbeyhill	NB	P	16.6.47
Leith Citadel – Junction Mills Sdg		F	5.2.68@
Junction Mills Sdg – Bonnington Goods Jn		F	28.2.68@
Bonnington Goods Jn – Bonnington South Jn		P	2.12.68@
Old Meldrum – Inverurie	GNS	P	2.11.31
		F	3.1.66@
Peebles – Symington	Cal	P	5.6.50
Peebles West – Broughton		F	7.6.54@
Broughton – Symington		F	4.4.66@
Penicuik – Roscwell & Hawthornden (Hawthornden Jn)	NB	P	10.9.51
		F	27.3.67@
Perth (Stanley Jn) – Laurencekirk (Kinnaber Jn) Cal		P	4.9.67
Forfar North Jn – Bridge of Dun		All	4.9.67@
Perth (Hilton Jn) – Cowdenbeath (North Jn)	NB	P	5.1.70
Bridge of Earn – Milnathort		All	5.1.70@
Milnathort – Kelty North Jn		F	4.5.70@
Kelty Coup – Cowdenbeath North Jn		F	12.7.72@
Peterhead – Maud Junction	GNS	P	3.5.65
		G	7.9.70@
Polton – Eskbank (Esk Valley Jn)	NB	P	10.9.51
		F	18.5.64@

Portobello (Niddrie North Jn) – Morningside Road –
    Edinburgh (Haymarket Central Jn)   NB P 10.9.62
    (Continued to be used on Sundays, Niddrie North Jn/
    Craiglockhart Jn/Slateford Jn, until 6.9.64)
Portpatrick – Stranraer Town   PPW P 6.2.50
    Portpatrick – Colfin   All 6.2.50@
    Colfin – Stranraer Town   F 1.4.59@
Possil – Partick West (East Jn/West Jn)   Cal P 5.10.64
    Partick North Jn – Partick East Jn   All 5.10.64@
    Possil – Partick West Jn   F 31.1.66@
Ratho (Low Level) – Kirkliston – Dalmeny (Jn) NB P 22.9.30
    Queensferry Jn – Kirkliston – Royal
    Elizabeth Yard   F 7.2.66@
Renfrew Porterfield – Cardonald Jn   G&P P 19.7.26
    Renfrew South No. 2 – Renfrew King's Inch   F 6.7.64@
    Renfrew King's Inch – Deanside   F ? @
Renfrew Wharf – Arkleston Jn   P 5.6.67
Riccarton Junction – Hexham (Border   NB P 15.10.56
    Counties Jn)
    Riccarton Junction – Bellingham (North Tyne) F 1.9.58@
    Bellingham (North Tyne) – Reedsmouth   F 11.11.63@
    Reedsmouth – Border Counties Jn   F 1.9.58@
Rosewell & Hawthornden – Eskbank   NB P 10.9.62
    (Hardengreen Jn)   F 27.3.67@
Rosewell & Hawthornden – Peebles – Galashiels   P 5.2.62
    (Kilnknowe Jn)
    Rosewell & Hawthornden – Hawthornden Jn F 27.3.67@
    Hawthornden Jn – Peebles – Kilnknowe Jn   All 5.2.62@
St Andrews – Leven   NB P 6.9.65
    St Andrews – Crail   F 5.10.64
    Crail – Leven   6.9.65@
                                  F 18.7.66@
St Boswells (Ravenswood Jn) – Duns   NB P 13.8.48
    Ravenswood Jn – Greenlaw   F 19.7.65@
    Greenlaw – Duns (flood damage)   All 13.8.48@
St Combs – Fraserburgh   GNS P 3.5.65@
                                  F 7.11.60
Selkirk – Galashiels (Selkirk Jn)   NB P 10.9.51
    Selkirk – Netherdale Siding   F 2.11.64@
    Netherdale Siding – Selkirk Jn   F 3.10.66@
Shotts East – Westcraigs Jn   NB F 17.6.63@

South Queensferry – Dalmeny   NB P 14.1.29
    South Queensferry – Dalmeny Jn   F 6.11.67@
Stirling – Alloa – Dunfermline Lower (Touch NB P 7.10.68
    South Jn)   F 5.1.70@
    Touch North Jn – Touch South Jn
Stonehouse – Dalserf   Cal P 7.1.35
    Stonehouse East Jn – Canderside Sdgs   F 23.2.35@
    Canderside Sdgs – Dalserf   F 20.4.64@
Stranraer (Challoch Jn) – Dumfries   PPW/GSW P 14.6.65
    Challoch Jn – Maxwelltown (ICI Siding)   All 14.6.65@
Stranraer Town – Stranraer Harbour Jn PPW P 7.3.66
Strathaven Central – Hamilton (Strathaven Jn) Cal P 1.10.45
    Strathaven Central – High Blantyre   F 21.9.53@
    High Blantyre – Strathaven Jn   F 1.6.60@
Strathaven – Stonehouse   Cal P 4.10.65@
    Strathaven Central – Stonehouse   F 7.12.64
Strathpeffer – Dingwall (Fodderty Jn) High P 23.2.46
                                  F 26.3.51@
Tayport – Leuchars Junction   NB P 9.1.56
    Leuchers Old – Spinning Mill Sdg   All 9.1.56@
    Leuchers Old – Leuchars Junction   F @
    Tayport – Spinning Mill Sdg   F 23.5.66@
Tayport – Newport-on-Tay East   NB All 23.5.66@
    (Temporary Closure, bus service 22.5.66 until finally closed P
    18.12.67)
Turnberry – Ayr (Alloway Jn)   GSW P 1.12.30
    (Reopened 1947, Heads of Ayr (Butlin's Camp) – Alloway Jn)
    Turnberry – Heads of Ayr (Butlin's Camp) F 28.2.55@
Turnberry – Girvan   GSW P 2.3.42
                                  F 28.2.55@
Uplawmoor – Neilston High   Cal P 2.4.62
                                  14.12.64@
Wanlockhead – Elvanfoot   Cal All 2.1.39@
Whifflet Upper – Langloan West Jn   Cal P 5.10.64
Whiteinch Victoria Park – Jordanhill NB P 2.4.51
                                  F 6.2.67@
Whithorn – Newton Stewart   PPW P 25.9.50
                                F 5.10.64@
Wilsontown – Auchengray (Wilsontown Jn) Cal P 10.9.51
                                F 4.5.64@

BIBLIOGRAPHY

British Branch Lines H. A. Vallance   *Batsford 1965*
The Glasgow & South Western Railway Campbell Highet
                                   Oakwood 1965
Preserved Locomotives H. C. Casserley   *Ian Allan 1968*
Light Railway Handbook R. W. Kidner   *Oakwood 1971*
Railway Magazine and Railway World – Various issues